# NATIVE ARTISTS of AFRICA

## Reavis Moore

**John Muir Publications**
Santa Fe, New Mexico

Dedicated to my children, Cisco and Cordelia

Special thanks to the artists, Malika Baikkou, David Dale, Wobayhu Werwero, Nangura Kungore, and Tsepo Tshola, and their families for sharing their lives with me.

John Muir Publications, P.O. Box 613, Santa Fe, New Mexico 87504

First edition. Second printing April 1995.
             First TWG printing December 1993.

Library of Congress Cataloging-in-Publication Data
Native artists of Africa  /  by Reavis Moore.
    p.    cm.
    Includes index.
ISBN  1-56261-147-X  :  $14.95 (hardcover)
ISBN  1-56261-229-8  :  $9.95 (paperback)
1. Artists—Africa—Biography—Juvenile literature.  2.  Arts, African—Juvenile literature.
[1. Arts, African. 2. Artists. 3. Blacks—Biography.] I. Title. II. Series.
NX587.M66  1994
700'.92'26—dc20                                                    93-6455
[B]                                                                CIP
                                                                   AC

Typefaces: Benguiat, Kabel
Illustrations: Chris Brigman
Design/Typography: Ken Wilson
Printer: Guynes Printing Company
Bindery: Prizma Industries, Inc.

Distributed to the book trade by
Publishers Group West
Emeryville, California

Distributed to the education market by
Wright Group Publishing, Inc.
19201 120th Avenue N.E.
Bothell, Washington 98011

# CONTENTS

# FOREWORD BY LEVAR BURTON

What is creativity? I'm sure it means something different to almost everyone, so I'll give you my definition. Creativity is that brilliant spark of life inside of me that I express in the world. How I express that creative spark is what defines me as an artist, whether its acting or writing or telling someone how I feel in a conversation.

You might feel creative when you're painting, singing, playing basketball, or cooking. My point is this: there is no one way to be creative. Creativity has as many faces as there are human beings on the planet. It is the job of the artist to discover what form of expression suits her or him best and then create from a place of joy. That is the key. We know we are on the creative path when what we do brings us joy.

Have you ever noticed how your own moods tend to affect those around you? How your good mood can help cheer up your best friend when he or she is feeling sad? The same is true when we express ourselves creatively. As artists, when we create from that place of pure joy, we have the ability to inspire those around us to discover their own creative spark. This is the miracle of creativity. This is how we change the world.

In the Rainbow Warrior Artists series you will meet remarkable individuals from around the world. You will hear them talk about creativity and how they express it in their lives. It is my hope that their stories will help fan your creative spark into a brilliant flame that helps to light the way for all of us.

# INTRODUCTION

**T**his is the second book in the Rainbow Warrior Artists series. The series is about native artists from around the world. In this book we visit five native African artists. One is a rug weaver, one a painter, one a dancer, one a basket weaver, and one a singer. Each of them is a creator. They create because they feel a need to express their thoughts and feelings. Being an artist comes naturally to each of them.

They also create art because they have a desire and feel a responsibility to maintain traditional tribal art. This art has been handed down to them from generation to generation since ancient tribal times. In the past, singing, dancing and making art were a part of everyday life, not professions. Today's Africa is very different from those times, but each of these artists feels a special connection to the past. Their art is a doorway that leads to their people's past.

The art that each of these artists creates is beautiful and graceful. But they all have experienced difficulties over the years in becoming artists. Their love of beauty and belief in the creative spirit have inspired them to continue, not just for themselves but for everyone who is touched and uplifted by their art.

I spent almost two months traveling from the north of Africa to its southern tip to meet and interview these artists. Africa is a place that words and pictures can never fully describe. Not only did I meet the five artists featured in this book, I met many other artists with great talents. Many of them lived simply, with little money and many difficulties in their lives. Others were well known and made lots of money from their art. What they all have in common is love for others, humility about their artistic skills, and a sense of joy that comes from creating art.

It is impossible to describe these artists in great detail in a few pages. But this book will introduce you to the history of each artist's people as well as to the artists themselves, their art, and their reasons for becoming artists. At the end of each chapter are suggestions on how you can create your own art similar to that made by the artists. I hope that these words and photos will bring their stories to life for you. My greatest wish is that a spark from their fires will land in your heart and set your being ablaze with your own creativity.

## WHAT TRIBE ARE YOU FROM?

We are all descendants of tribal cultures. In the past, your ancestors lived in tribes in Europe, North America, South America, Africa, Asia, or elsewhere. Many of the values the artists in this book express, such as respect for the Earth, were sacred to your ancestors as well. This book may inspire you to discover your own tribal heritage and explore your own traditions.

For instance, if your ancestors were European, you may be a descendant of the Celtic *(KEL-tik)* tribe. The Celts were almost destroyed by foreign armies and religions. But Celtic storytelling, music, dancing, and seasonal celebrations live on in parts of Ireland, Scotland, England, and continental Europe. Even a form of the ancient language is still spoken.

As we enter the twenty-first century, we face questions about our survival. Remembering our past and the values that were important to our ancestors may help us prepare for the challenges of the future.

And now, let's enter the world of African artists.

# MALIKA BAIKKOU
## of the Berber People

### THE BERBER LAND AND PEOPLE

**S**outh of Spain on the other side of the Mediterranean Sea is the continent of Africa and the ancient, magical country of Morocco. In the eastern part of Morocco are the Atlas Mountains. These mountains are the traditional homeland of the Berber *(BER-ber)* people. Berbers are the original inhabitants of this country. Today, they make up 70 percent of the population of Morocco.

The story of the Berber people is one of bravery against invaders, both European and Arab. The Arabs invaded the Berbers nearly 500 years ago and forced them to convert to Islam, the religion of the Moslems. The French controlled all of Morocco from the 1800s until the 1940s. Today, Morocco is again ruled by a king of Arab descent. But despite their political struggles, Berbers have maintained a peaceful, lush mountain paradise where they produce abundant food and have large, stable families.

*The Berber village of Ben Smem*

"**W**hen I am weaving I forget everything else. I concentrate completely on the work and the pattern I must follow. The great happiness comes when I finish it."

—Malika Baikkou

Most Berbers live in villages of a few hundred people. These villages usually sit in small mountain valleys. The houses are made of mud or stone and are built on the gently sloping sides of the valleys. At the bottom of the valleys are fields and orchards where grains, vegetables, and fruits are grown. The boundaries between the fields are marked by curving walls of piled stones. Usually a stream or a water canal runs through the village to the fields. The hills around the village are crisscrossed with well-worn trails the villagers use to travel to fields farther away or to a nearby village or town.

One of the first things you notice about a Berber village is the Moslem mosque and prayer tower. Even tiny villages have a mosque at their center. Twice a day, at 4:00 a.m. and again in the evening, loudspeakers in the tower call the people to prayer. Most Berbers now consider themselves Moslems. Whatever remains of the traditional religion is now part of how they practice Islam.

*Berber woman and child*

Walking into a traditional Berber village is like walking back in time. Most people begin work before the sun comes up. But the work is done at an unhurried pace. The Berbers' farming produces an abundance of fresh foods and also a deep sense of belonging and connection to the land. This way of life has developed over many centuries as one generation after another improved living conditions in the village. Although today some of the villages have electricity, and some of

the homes have televisions, the old ways continue. The men tend their green fields and orchards. The women weave brilliantly colored rugs and cook for the families. From about noon to 2:00 p.m., all work stops in the village as people go inside for food, tea, and rest.

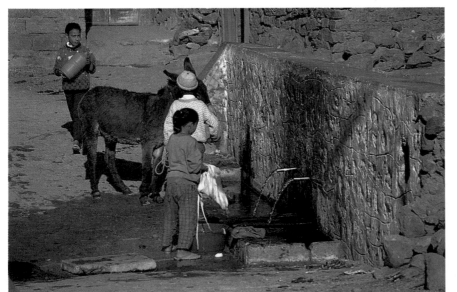

*A Berber village spring*

## MALIKA BAIKKOU

Malika Baikkou *(MAH-lee-kah BAH-koo)* lives in the Berber village of Ben Smem in the Atlas Mountains in north-eastern Morocco. The name Malika means "queen." She was born in 1974 and has spent her whole life in Ben Smem.

*I was born in this house, and I have lived all my 19 years here.*

Generations of her family, like most families here, have lived in the village longer than anyone can remember.

*Father before father before father was here in this village. My family has been here for a long, long time.*

Malika's life has been completely centered on her family and her village. Before being interviewed for this book she had never spoken to, or even met, a person from another country. When she was a child she played with girls and boys. But after the age of ten, girls and boys no longer play together.

*Malika (right) and friend*

This is because Moslem law separates men and women in very specific ways. Malika began school when she was seven years old. There she learned the Arabic and French languages.

*I enjoyed French more. I found Arabic grammar difficult, but I learned them both.*

Today she is fluent in three languages, including her native Berber tongue.

*I liked school and being with the other children. But when I was 12 my father decided it was time for me to stay at home and help my mother and learn from her.*

This part of her education focused on homemaking skills, such as sewing clothes for the family and cooking. Preparing and cooking food

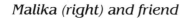

*Children in the village*

Malika weaving a rug

takes up much time in a Berber woman's day. With few appliances and no running water, Malika and her mother can spend much of their day preparing meals for the family.

Malika is a Moslem, but her way of life is Berber.

*Before Islam came here there was no (formal) religion. But we are free to believe whatever we want, and our Berber traditions are still practiced.*

As part of the Islamic tradition Malika occasionally makes pilgrimages to visit holy men in other parts of Morocco. The purpose of these visits is to honor the holy man as well as to seek his blessing. Malika dreams of one day visiting other parts of the world  including the United States and Europe.

*I dream about traveling abroad. America seems like such a big place. For me it's only pictures on TV.*

Malika has a daughter named Souad *(soo-AHD)*. Like so many other mothers around the world, she is single. But she will probably marry soon, since the family is looking for a young man for her. Although her father and mother may suggest someone for her to marry, in the end it is up to her to decide.

*When I marry, everyone in the village will be invited and we will have a party for two nights.*

## WEAVING THE RUG OF LIFE

As a child Malika played a game using very long pieces of wool yarn. This game, played by many Berber children, was designed long ago to help the women rug weavers. In the game the children wind up yarn into little wooden containers that look like rattles.

*I knew from the time I was very small that I wanted to become a weaver. It was the best thing for me to do, and I have benefited from it in many ways.*

When Malika left school she began to spend much of her time with her mother and other women, learning rug weaving.

*My mother was my first teacher of weaving. Then some of the older women from the village helped me. My friends and I then continued and helped each other to do the weaving. I started weaving when I was about ten. By the time I was 13 I could make a carpet by myself.*

These rugs are woven on large looms. Often two or three women work together on a rug. Certain types of rugs are woven for special occasions like weddings and births. If the family and village have a good harvest, a special rug will be woven that has silver sequins on it. This is a symbol of wealth.

*Before I start the carpet, I imagine what it will look like. If good things are happening in the village, like a lot of rain for the crops, then I make a different, special kind of carpet.*

Weaving a carpet is a very slow process and requires many different steps.

*First, I wash the line. Then I have one of the older people dye the lines different colors from natural plant dyes. Sometimes I go to pray before I start weaving.*

The weaving is done in her home or in the home of a friend. After the preparations are complete, the long process of weaving begins.

*A traditional Berber rug*

*One of Malika's rugs*

*A Berber woman weaving on a loom*

Sometimes it takes many months to complete a rug.

*When I finally start weaving I feel very happy. But I also know how difficult it will be and how much time it will take. When I am weaving I forget everything else. I concentrate completely on the work and the pattern I must follow. It's like painting a picture. The great happiness comes when I finish it! This is always a happy day for me.*

The rugs are woven for use by the family, or to be given away as gifts. Others are sold at the market to help support the family.

*I keep some of my carpets, and some I sell for money. But each one I make with the same care and love.*

When Malika is weaving on the loom she seems much older than her years. You can feel the presence of her ancestors who have woven in the same way for so many centuries. Weaving brings Malika great joy.

*I make something beautiful from natural things. I love my work.*

## PEACE, LOVE, AND FREEDOM FOR ALL CHILDREN

Many of us take education for granted. How many times have you wished you didn't have to go to school? Malika believes that education is the key to a fuller life and greater freedom.

*I never had a chance to finish my studies. I hope that everyone who reads this book will stay with their studies, even when it's hard. Later, you'll be glad that you did.*

Equally important to her is the continuation of her tribal traditions.

*I want my daughter to learn what I didn't have a chance to learn. But also I want to teach her how to make carpets. My dream is that the art of weaving and the other traditions won't disappear from the villages. To the boys I say, I hope you don't forget about creativity. I think for girls it's easier to try creative things. But I don't want the creativity of men to disappear from the world just because they have to take jobs.*

The next time your parents tell you something you don't want to hear, remember these words from Malika.

*Find out what your father and mother know. There is so much you can learn from them, and they won't always be there to help you.*

The world that Malika lives in may be very different from yours, but her desire for beauty and a good life are the same as yours. She offers this wish for you, wherever you live.

*I want all the people in the world to be free from war. And I wish peace and love and freedom for all children in the world.*

## WEAVING

You can make a woven bookmark or belt by following these simple steps.

You will need the following things:
- 4 drinking straws.
- 4 pieces of heavy twine, each about 24 inches long.
- 3 pieces of differently colored yarn, each about 36" long.

**Step 1.** Thread a piece of the twine through each straw. Tie a knot at the bottom of each piece of twine.

**Step 2.** Tie the pieces of twine together at the top.

**Step 3.** Tie a piece of yarn to the outside piece of twine near the top of the straw. This will anchor it in place as you weave. Now, weave the yarn over and under the straws, back and forth until you come to the end of the yarn. As you weave, push the yarn up so the weave is tight.

**Step 4.** Now tie a differently colored piece of yarn to the piece of yarn woven around the straws. Just like you did before, weave this new piece of yarn over and under the straws. When you finish, repeat this step with the third piece of yarn. You can make your weaving as long as you want by tying on additional pieces of twine (see illustration).

**Step 5.** When you are done weaving, push the yarn over the tops of the straws and set the straws aside. Tie the two pieces of twine on the left together with a double knot. Then tie the two pieces on the right together the same way. Tie the two center strands of twine together with a double knot. Finally, tie the right and left strands together the same way. You can glue buttons, sequins, or other decorations to your weaving to make it more colorful.

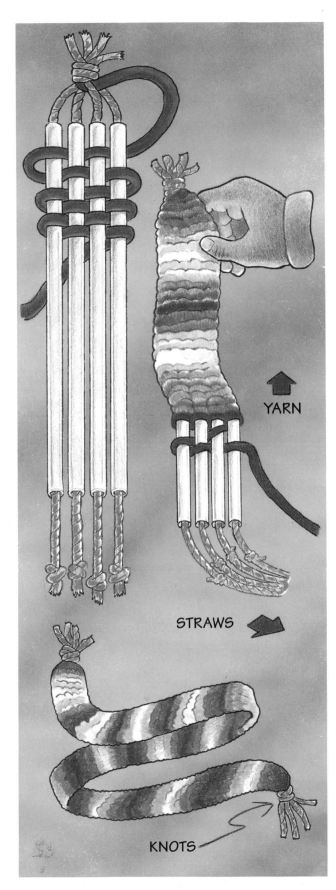

YARN

STRAWS

KNOTS

# DAVID DALE
## of the Itshekiri Tribe

### THE ITSHEKIRI LAND AND PEOPLE

On the west coast of Africa, close to the equator, is the nation of Nigeria. Nigeria is the wealthiest and most highly populated country in Africa.

One of the oldest tribes of Nigeria is the Itshekiri *(EAT-shah-kir-ee)*. These people live in the delta state on the coast of southern Nigeria. There are many rivers in their tribal lands. They all flow into the Atlantic Ocean. The Itshekiri feel a deep connection to the water. They believe that their ancient ancestors originally came from the sea and that when members of the tribe die their spirits return there. They pray to their ancestors and make offerings to the rivers and the sea as a way of communicating with those who lived before them.

The Itshekiri know how to read signs in nature to predict future events. For example, they study the clouds, moon, stars, and the movements of animals to predict when it will next rain.

*"If you find the rhythm of life, you will never be off the beat. One very important part of that rhythm is the golden rule: treat others the way you want them to treat you."*

—David Dale

Freida High W. Tesfagiorgis

A traditional artisan dyeing clothing

14

Each year the people celebrate a series of festivals related to nature. One is the yam festival, which happens after the harvesting of the yam, an important food for the Itshekiri. The people believe that before they eat any of the yams they should honor the food. So they hold a festival where they perform ceremonies and pray before feasting on the yams.

The Itshekiri grow crops and raise animals for food. They also still fish in the sea and hunt wild animals as their ancestors did. Some of the animals they hunt are the antelope, the civet (a wild cat), the boar, and very large land snails.

These people are proud that they were among the first tribes in west Africa to make contact with the Europeans hundreds of years ago. This is startling since European and American slave traders carried away hundreds of thousands of African people from this area.

Today, the traditional way of life of the Itshekiri people is still practiced by

*Drummers in traditional dress*

many people, but it is now usually mixed together with European ideas and habits. Some of the people now reject their traditional culture. Others reject the new ways. But for most Itshekiri, traditional tribal religion and Christianity have combined to form a unique blend of old and new.

Many of the tribe members have migrated to large cities such as Lagos in order to find work. Once there, the old ways are often forgotten or become lost in the rush of modern city life and the struggle to survive.

*The Lagos skyline*

15

## DAVID DALE

David Dale was born in Kano, Nigeria, in 1946. His mother is from the Itshekiri tribe and his father is British.

David grew up living in two worlds. Throughout most of his childhood he divided his time between Nigeria and England. This unique upbringing gave him the best of both cultures. In Nigeria he learned the traditional creative ways of his people and developed his connection with the Earth. His mother shared with him her ability to see the future by reading signs in nature. In England he lived with his father's sister, who is an author and an avid gardener. There, he studied art and benefited from a strong school education.

*From the time I was three until I was 17, I went back and forth between Nigeria and England. I think I grew up too quickly, but I think it was good for me. Having dark skin in England wasn't always easy, but sometimes it was funny. On very cold school days, other boys and I would come in from outside and go to the water closet (restroom) and look in the mirror to see who had the whitest skin from being in the cold. I never won that game!*

In his heart David always knew that Nigeria was his home.

*Because of my interest in my African culture and traditions, I knew that one day I would stay in Nigeria full-time. But another reason I knew I would live here is because I don't like winters very much.*

In 1963 he came home to Nigeria to attend the university. His first year he rented a house, which he later bought, near the center of Lagos.

Lagos is one of the largest cities in Africa. To an

*David (left) and his friends*

*A marketplace in Lagos*

*Nigerian boys*

American it might seem wild and out of control. The sidewalks are filled with people talking loudly, often arguing and spilling out into the street. Many of the people are very poor. The streets are packed with thousands of cars, and people drive so fast it seems like there are no traffic laws. Horns are always honking and radios blaring. The city feels like it's about to burst at the seams.

It has been thirty years since David first came to Lagos, and he still lives and works in the same house. His house is surrounded by beautiful flowers and plants. Inside, the rooms are overflowing with art and art in progress. From morning to night, David is surrounded by young assistants who greatly respect him and are anxious to help him in any way they can.

Since his childhood, David has had the gift of clairvoyance.

*I know when very good or bad things are going to happen to people close to me. I see it in a dream or I have body signs. For example, if I have a twitch on the lower eye lid, it means that someone close to me is going to die soon. That happens very rarely. At the age of seven these things had already been formed in me.*

Without words David communicates love and peace. His kindness and openness are felt the moment he walks into a room. The contrast between the poverty and chaos on the streets of Lagos and the calm and creativity of David's world shows how much impact just one person can have. It is as though he is slowly and quietly building an island of peace and art in the stormy sea of a turbulent city.

## BORN TO BE AN ARTIST

David is an artist who works with many types of materials. He draws and paints with oil paints, watercolors, pencils, and charcoal. He etches and engraves wood. He also uses beads, metal foils, and stained glass. His artistic gifts have been a part of him all his life.

*At the age of three I became very aware of colors. By the time I was seven I was winning prizes for my art in school. When I was 12 I won my first medal in an international art contest.*

David and his assistants glue colored beads on a board to make an artwork like the one at right

But despite his obvious talents and his desire to develop his art, like many other artists, he found that his parents didn't agree with his career choice.

*When I went to the university I had a big problem with my family. They said I should become a banker or pharmacist. I wanted to study art. They had plenty of money to send me to the university, but because I wouldn't take the courses they wanted me to they wouldn't sponsor me. So I had to work my way through school from the age of 17. But while I was doing temporary office work for the government, I designed a logo for the ministry of communications. They liked it so much that they gave me enough money to pay my tuition and buy books for several years.*

David sees a vision of his art in his mind before he uses materials to give it form.

*Before I create a piece of art I can see exactly what I want to do. I know what it's going to be.*

David is a Christian and he believes his talent comes from something much greater than himself.

*When I am creating I reach a stage where the fingers are moving, but it's not me that's doing it. That's when I know it's the essence of God that's over me. I can't control it, I just know that it's moving me. It's then I tell myself, "He's taken over from you."*

"Lobsters and Fishes," made from etching on linoleum

18

Freida High W. Tesfagiorgis

*A beaded artwork called "Leopard in Cornfield"*

David has traveled from his own internal world of ideas and vision to the wide world around him. He is now considered to be one of the most important African artists of his time.

*My art has taken me to many places. I've been to all the Nordic countries. I've had shows in Germany, Holland, France, Italy, England and Belgium. During the peak of Communism, I traveled with a Nigerian art exhibition throughout Eastern Europe. I've had shows in the U.S., Canada, Cuba, Brazil, Japan, and other countries in Africa.*

He is currently preparing a series of exhibitions for his fiftieth birthday in 1996. At these shows he will display all of his different types of artwork.

*I believe very much in humanity, so the main themes of these exhibitions will be peace, love, and harmony.*

David has never really doubted what he should do with his life. He was born to be an artist. But after he's finished with his work here, he has another career in mind.

*If I had to be born again, I would do exactly what I've done all over again. But I'm not coming back! I intend to stay in God's garden and water His roses.*

## LEARN THE RHYTHM OF LIFE

David loves children. In many ways he has kept his childhood alive in his heart. His ideas on living may help you to better understand what's happening in your own life.

*Study closely the feelings and desires that enter your heart. Decide if they are going to help you be happy or cause you trouble. Then you'll be able to decide for yourself whether to cultivate them or weed them out. That philosophy has guided me to where I am today.*

The difficulties he had making his parents understand his artistic nature have given him some very strong ideas about how to treat children.

*To the parents I say, don't be too fussy. Encourage the children. Let them decide for themselves what they want to do. I don't think anything should be forced on children. Children, you have your own glorious developing to do.*

David's success and happiness come from his feeling for life. He believes there is a rhythm to living.

*If you find the rhythm of life, you will never be off the beat. One very important part of that rhythm is the golden rule: treat others the way you want them to treat you.*

Regardless of what you choose to do with your life, you will have to face the problems that come with living. In the midst of your difficulties find a way to feel peaceful and loving. If you are having trouble in your life, you might want to carry David's words with you.

*My message to the children is, don't keep anger. Show love. It makes for better sunshine and better laughter.*

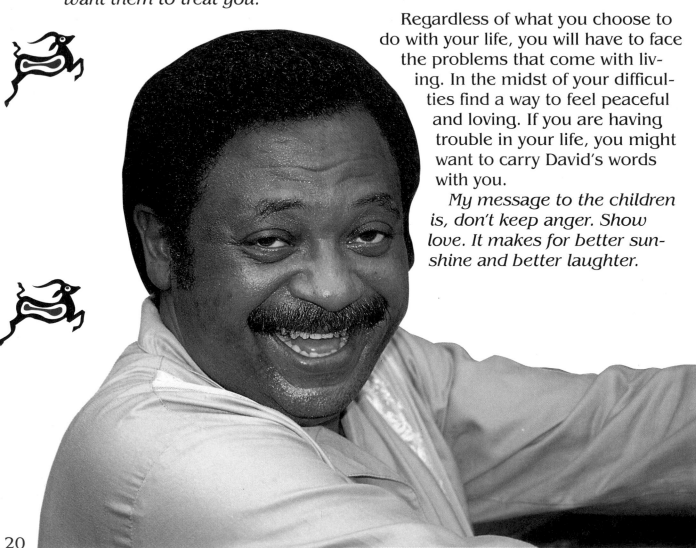

## DRAW WHAT YOU SEE IN YOUR MIND

David always sees his artwork in his mind before he makes it. You can too! You don't have to be an artist, you just have to be willing to try and try again.

You will need the following things:

- A sharp pencil.
- Some pieces of white paper.

**Step 1.** Find a quiet place, preferably in nature, where you can draw. Take some time to picture in your mind what you want to draw. Pick a favorite thing, like a friend's face, your pet, or something in your room. Think carefully about all the lines and shapes it has. Think carefully about what lines you need to draw to create its image on the paper. Don't hurry this step. If you are having difficulty, try to picture something different in your mind.

**Step 2.** With the picture clearly in your mind, draw a simple outline of it. Go slowly. Don't be afraid to erase or start over if you need to.

**Step 3.** Now add details to the outline that fill in the center of your picture. Continue to study your mental image as you draw.

**Step 4.** After you have completed your picture take time to think about how close it looks to the picture in your mind. Decide how you could do it differently. Now try it again. Start with an outline, then fill in the details. Are you having fun? Maybe you, too, will grow up to become an artist.

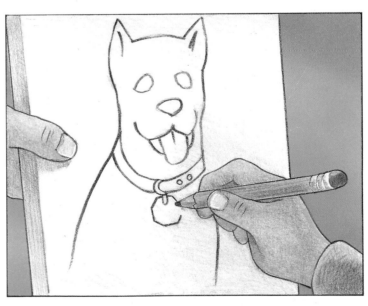

# WOBAYHU WERWERO
## of the Gurage Tribe

### THE GURAGE LAND AND PEOPLE

The Gurage *(goo-RAH-gee)* tribe lives in northeastern Africa in the country of Ethiopia. The name Gurage means "belonging to the left," because the people migrated to the "left," or southward, from the village of Gura. Today, their homeland is in southern Ethiopia. Their lands are dotted with green hills and mountains. They live in beautiful valleys along rivers and streams as well as in the highlands. One of the largest rivers in Ethiopia, the Omo, serves as the western border of their lands.

Most of the Gurage people are farmers. Among other things they grow cabbage, potatoes, wheat, barley, mangoes, papayas, bananas, and a plant called *ensete*, which means "false banana." The leaves and roots of the ensete, which does not bear fruit, are used to make a flour from which the people make bread, one of the main foods of the

"*When I dance I am really happy. I am filled with real feelings. Something deep inside of me comes alive.*"

—Wobayhu Werwero

*Traditional Gurage homes*

tribe. The weather is never very cold. Most years, there is plenty of rain and the skies are filled with rainbows. The growing season is long and bountiful.

Most people walk or use animals for transportation. There are few cars. Buses make daily trips from the villages to the larger towns and cities.

People live in traditional houses of mud and stone with pointed straw roofs. The houses are clustered together in small communities. Large families made up of great-grandparents, grandparents, parents, uncles, aunts, children, and cousins share several houses grouped together.

The women weave colorful baskets in many shapes to be used for serving and storing food. The people celebrate and pass on their history and values from one generation to the next through songs and stories. Certain people of each generation memorize these songs and stories. They sing the songs and tell the stories at many tribal and family gatherings. They also teach them to their children, so the history will be remembered. Until recently, none of these songs and stories were recorded in writing.

*A Gurage child*

The Gurage people also have complex traditional dances for religious worship and social occasions such as marriages. Their traditional clothing ranges from simple white cotton for daily wear to embroidered costumes for ceremonies and celebrations.

The Gurage people have probably lived in Ethiopia for more than 2,000 years. Some believe they moved to the south from northern Ethiopia about 500 years ago. Others believe they've been in the south for more than 2,000 years. They may have originally migrated across the Red Sea from the lands that are now Saudi Arabia and Yemen. Throughout their history the Gurage have held a deep respect for nature and its seasons.

Their ancient religious beliefs speak of Wok (the sky god), Boza (the thunder god), and Damauwit (the fertility goddess). They are all children of the supreme god, Yigser. It is believed that he gave supernatural powers to his children to guide the Gurage society and provide them with rain, rich harvests, health, and victory over their enemies. Annual religious festivals are held at two shrines in ancient pine and eucalyptus forests. One of these festivals is in honor of Damauwit, who is the protector of Gurage womanhood. Each January thousands of women come together at these sacred sites to sing and dance to honor the goddess.

In modern times many Gurage people have moved from the villages to Ethiopian cities such as the capital, Addis Ababa. But even in the cities the Gurage band together to form small villages within the cities.

## WOBAYHU WERWERO

Wobayhu Werwero *(woh-BUY-you wee-WER-oh)* is a traditional Gurage dancer. Her parents and grandparents originally lived in the town of Waliso in the Gurage lands. In the 1960s her parents moved to Addis Ababa, where Wobayhu was born in 1970. She is the sixth child and has five brothers and five sisters. The children have lived all of their lives in Addis Ababa, but all members of the family take part in Gurage traditional life. Wobayhu, however, is the only one who has dedicated her work and her life to the creative expression of Gurage traditions.

Even though she grew up in a city Wobayhu has never been far from her tribal roots.

*My family is part of a community or village of Gurages who live together in the same area of the city. Many of the old ways continue, including dancing and singing. As a village we come together often to celebrate our traditions, so they will not be forgotten. We live in the middle of a big city with people from many places, but we always remember that we are Gurage.*

Wobayhu and her family, along with other families, carry on much of the social and cultural life that is found in a tribal village. Tribal stories are passed down, religious rituals continue, Gurage foods are carefully prepared, and traditional dress is still worn on important occasions. She also takes trips to the Gurage lands for weddings and to visit relatives there.

The influences of modern culture, however, have found their way into Wobayhu's life. She went to public schools, wears western-style clothing, and has never really experienced the farming life that is at the heart of the Gurage way. But in the city she has had the opportunity to learn about the traditions of other Ethiopian

*A Gurage village*

tribal cultures as well as about the ways of the world outside her country.

*I like traditional music and listen to tapes of Gurage songs, but I also listen and dance to modern music. As a child I liked to play with the boys. Especially, I liked to play soccer with them.*

Dancing was also a big part of Wobayhu's childhood. She spent a lot of time with her grandmother, who was her first dance teacher.

*When I was very young I asked my grandmother to help me learn the dances. She taught me a very traditional Gurage dance that she knew. That was what really got me started.*

For the Gurage people, dancing is not something separate from daily life. It is an important part of everyone's life. On any weekend, in any Gurage

A Gurage woman weaving a basket

village or town, even in the cities, you are likely to hear the sounds of clapping and singing at a Gurage wedding. The people dress in beautiful, embroidered white clothing as they dance in celebration of the continuation of the family life. The festivities and the dancing go on for hours, sometimes days. This is where Wobayhu first developed her love for dance.

## LIVING TO DANCE

Dancing has always been Wobayhu's greatest passion. She knew at a very early age that she wanted to be a dancer.

*In the eighth grade I became very interested in dancing. Besides dancing at gatherings, I would listen to Gurage music and dance along. It was not hard for me because it had always been around me and I wanted to do it.*

Her dancing in the Gurage community village brought her to the attention of a government cultural youth group. At the age of 17 she was chosen to participate in a program sponsored by the Ethiopian ministry of culture. The program was the beginning of her formal training in traditional dance. In addition to the Gurage dances she also learned the dances of the other tribes of her country.

*The government was socialist at that time. They developed these cultural programs to promote the unity of all the people of Ethiopia. We gave public performances here and in other countries. But it was a chance for me to express myself and my traditions and a way to preserve the traditions. Most importantly, it was what I really wanted to do, to dance.*

*Wobayhu dancing*

Today, she is part of a troupe of professional dancers and is one of the most popular traditional dancers in Ethiopia. She has traveled within Ethiopia, to the United States, and throughout Europe to perform the dances of her people. Her dancing has helped to keep the traditional culture alive and thriving in a time when the survival of tribal traditions everywhere is being challenged by the modern way of life.

For Wobayhu, dancing is more than memorizing movements. It is also an expression of her joy.

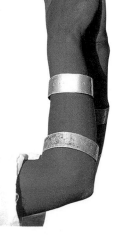

*When I dance I am really happy. I am filled with real feelings. Something deep inside of me comes alive.*

As in most cultures, Gurage dancing is usually done with a partner of the other sex. Wobayhu and her partner have been dancing together for six years. When they dance they are like one person. Each knows exactly what the other will do and when. Their dancing creates an excitement and energy around them that draws everyone who watches into the dance. Each of the dances has a specific purpose.

*At a wedding we do a dance where everyone makes a circle. The drum keeps the rhythm, and everyone claps and sings. This is an expression of joy for the people being married and brings blessings to them. It has been done this way for a long, long time.*

Wobayhu does not take the responsibility and privilege of dancing lightly. Before she performs, she and the other dancers in her troupe take time to pray and ask for guidance. This helps them remember the ancestors who danced before them. It helps them remember the importance of the dances they are about to perform.

*Traditional Gurage dance movement*

*Gurage ceremonial dress*

## MAKE YOURSELF HAPPY

Wobayhu's life story may help you to discover and develop your creative gifts. Doing so may help you find happiness and may inspire others to tap into their own creativity. Wobayhu faced many obstacles on her path to becoming a dancer. Her parents did not agree with her decision to make dancing her full-time occupation. But Wobayhu believed strongly in her decision. Her determination gave her the strength to pursue her goals. As you might find in your own life, an older person encouraged her to follow her dreams.

*Even though my parents did not want me to be a dancer, my grandmother believed in me, taught me, and is proud of me. Of course, my parents now can appreciate what I do, because I am successful at it.*

First, you must know what you want. You have to look closely at everything and everyone around you. Think carefully about your own special talents, the things that come most naturally to you. Think carefully about the kind of life you want to lead. Then you can begin to decide which direction to go in.

Whatever your dream is, whichever path you choose, you will have to overcome your own doubts and the doubts of others if you want to be successful. Everyone who has ever made their dreams come true has had to work hard and struggle for success. Sometimes when you are just beginning, it is hard to find the joy and inspiration to continue. But Wobayhu's words may help you to see that joy comes even from the struggles.

*I have nothing new to say. Just practice, rehearse whatever you do. That will make you happy, and eventually it will fill your whole life with happiness!*

## DANCING FOR JOY

Wobayhu knows a lot about dancing. She believes that the most important part of being a good dancer is to feel joyful while you are dancing. Follow these simple instructions and you, too, can dance for joy.

You will need the following things:
- A record, tape, or CD with music that makes you feel like dancing.
- Enough open space to dance in. You can dance alone or with a partner.

**Step 1.** Before playing the music, sit quietly and think about the things in your life that you are grateful for, such as your family, your friends, your teachers, and your home. Feel the appreciation and happiness building inside of you.

**Step 2.** Start the music. Stand up and stretch. Shake your arms, hands, feet, and legs. Get loose!

**Step 3.** Now, concentrate on the rhythm of the music and begin to move your feet back and forth to it. Let your arms hang down at your side.

**Step 4.** Keeping the rhythm with your feet, raise your hands up and touch your fingertips together. Now pull your fingertips back and touch your palms together. Again touch your fingertips together, then your palms. Repeat this movement to the rhythm of the music and start to bring your hands together hard enough to make a clapping sound. Continue doing this until you feel in harmony with the music.

**Step 5.** You may want to play the same song over several times. An important part of most traditional dancing is doing the same movements over and over. Think of other movements to add to your dance. For example, first put your hands on your hips. Then bring your fingers together, clap your palms together, and return your hands to your hips. What other movements can you add? Remember, always listen closely to the rhythm of the music. Move your body to the music's rhythm and feel joyful.

# NANGURA KUNGORE
## of the Mbukushu Tribe

### THE MBUKUSHU LAND AND PEOPLE

In the south-central part of Africa is the country of Botswana. Once a British colony, today Botswana is an independent nation and one of the most stable and prosperous countries in Africa. It is also home to a large, protected population of wildlife.

One of the native tribes that lives in Botswana is the Mbukushu (m' buh-KOO-shoo). They belong to a group of tribes known collectively as Bantu, which means "the people." The Mbukushu originally lived in central Africa. Over many centuries they migrated south to Zambia, then to southern Angola and northern Namibia. In the mid-1960s a part of the tribe fled the civil war in Namibia and came as refugees to Botswana, where they settled and reestablished their culture.

The Mbukushu tribe has an ancient relationship with the wild animals of this part of Africa. This relationship is very important to them.

*"I want the children to learn, so that they can know the good way of life. Education is important."*

—Nangura Kungore

*Zebras in Botswana*

Their myths and folklore are filled with tales of the zebra, the springbok (a type of gazelle), the giraffe, and the lion. Even the lowly porcupine has a place of honor. Its pointy pelt is worn in healing ceremonies by the tribal medicine men. When a great hippopotamus is killed, its bounty is shared by the whole village. Only the chief, however, is allowed to slay the animal and divide up the carcass.

The greatest of all the animals in the Mbukushu world is the elephant. Its name alone fills the people with fear and awe. Before guns became available to the tribespeople, they rarely, if ever, hunted the great beast and did not know what elephant meat tasted like. Because of this, one tribal story says that in the elephant you will find meats that taste like all the other kinds of animals and fishes.

Before Christianity was introduced to the area, the Mbukushu tribe had no formal religious practices or ceremonies. Still, they led spiritual lives and treated all life as sacred. Even today, they kill only what they need to survive. They continue to celebrate the arrival of the seasons and the migrations of the animals.

*Reeds used for weaving baskets*

The Mbukushu believe that Nyambi, the Creator, created the world and set everything in motion. After that, he removed himself from direct contact with the world. The Mbukushu believe that the spirits of their dead ancestors can communicate Nyambi's will to living people as well as carry the wishes of the people back to him.

One tribal story says that the first person was sent down from heaven by Nyambi and arrived on Earth in the Sabelo hills. According to the legend you can still see the footprints in the rocks where the first person landed many thousands of years ago.

*Mbukushu children*

## NANGURA KUNGORE

Nangura Kungore (NAN-goo-rah koon-GORE-ee) lives in the small town of Etsha (ET-sah), which means "the pool that never dries up." The town sits on the edge of the great Okavango Delta, a swamp. Nangura was born in 1970. She has an infant daughter whose name is Ithobogeng (ee-koh-boh-HENG).

Nangura (right) and her sister

Nangura's home is in a village of about a dozen huts. The huts are made of mud, have thatched roofs, and are surrounded by open space. There is no electricity or plumbing, and Nangura doesn't mind.

*I don't want electricity. It is for the rich, not the poor. I like things the way they are.*

There is a peaceful, unhurried feeling in the village. People sit on the ground talking or weaving baskets. Children's laughter fills the air. Women walk slowly back and forth from a nearby well, balancing containers of water on their heads.

As a child Nangura attended a school with an English teacher called a headmaster. There, she learned to speak English with a slight British accent. The school draws students from different tribes in the area. For most of the students, it is their first exposure to the world outside their villages.

*Before I started school I didn't know anything. I was just living. Helping my father. I was a simple child.*

The school teaches more than just academic subjects. It also helps the students explore their traditions and culture. At night the sound of students singing, dancing, and drumming floats out from the campus to the surrounding villages. To Nangura, the most interesting part of her school years was the traditional dancing.

*At school we had a traditional dance group that performed and traveled to other towns to compete. When I*

Traditional Mbukushu homes

Traditional Mbukushu dancers

was dancing there, we were picked as the best dancers from all the schools.

Basket weaving, however, was her greatest love.

Today, Nangura still lives in her village a few hundred yards from the school she attended. A typical day for her begins at 6:30 a.m.

*When I get up I put the water on the fire. Then I make porridge and tea for breakfast. I make hot water for my child and myself to bathe outside the house. Sometimes I leave my dishes dirty, and sometimes I don't make my bed. I just leave the blankets messy. At night I go to bed at 8:00 unless I am thinking about my life or about someone who is far from me. Then I may not go to sleep until 9:30.*

Nangura spends her days at a nearby artist's cooperative where she works with basket weavers, woodworkers, and other craftspeople who come there to sell their work.

*I like my work very much. I am helping people to make money to live. I look at their baskets, jewelry, thumb pianos (a hand-held instrument you play with your thumbs), and many other things, and I decide how much they should receive for them. I also weave baskets myself.*

Nangura and her daughter

33

## WEAVING BASKETS OF BEAUTY

Basket weaving

Nangura first learned about basket weaving when she was a child.

*I remember that when I was small, the women were weaving in my village. Many people here weave baskets. I started to weave when I was 12. I started to weave because it was simple for me. I asked my mother how to weave. My mother said, "This is our life to put the designs in the baskets." My art teacher at school really pushed me to start weaving on my own. Now I do three types of weaving, and I know four traditional designs.*

The inspiration for the basket patterns comes mainly from animals. The names of these patterns present a beautiful picture of African wildlife. "Flight of the swallow," "tears of the giraffe," "running ostrich," "knees of the tortoise," and "back of the python" are just a few.

Like the Mbukushu, tribes around the world developed basket weaving to improve their lives and chances for survival.

*Traditionally, we carry and store grains, peanuts, sorghum, and different foods in the baskets. If you go to the bush for fruits, you can carry them back in the basket. We store seeds in the closed baskets.*

Since the Mbukushu came in contact with white people and their modern ways, traditional basket weaving has declined. In recent years, however, more people have rediscovered weaving as a way to make money. The baskets that Nangura and her people make are still used for traditional purposes, but today they are also made to trade and sell.

*The white people buy the baskets, and we get the money to buy things we need. The basket is very important for the black people. If I get money for my baskets I can get a dress for my child and buy sorghum, soap, and everything we need for our lives.*

Nangura preparing to weave

*Mbukushu baskets*

Making a basket takes a long time and involves many steps. The finished basket is an example of nature's gifts lovingly used to create something beautiful and practical.

*Before I weave I go to the river to get the palm leaves that we use to make the baskets and to find the dye trees. We use the bark, root, and leaves of the trees to make colors to dye the palm leaves. There are three types of trees. We use one to make black dye, one to make red, and one to make purple dye. We boil the parts of the trees in water and then put the leaves in until they take the color.*

*As I am making the basket I follow a pattern that I have in my mind. Sometimes it is a traditional pattern. Sometimes it is something new that I make up myself. I also think about my life. If I am suffering, I think about what I should do.*

Sitting in the sun or the shade of a tree, Nangura carefully weaves the colored leaves together. It is peaceful work. Sometimes she works alone quietly. Other times women sit together talking and laughing as they weave. For Nangura the rush of the modern world is far away, and the presence of the past is felt as she performs the weaving motion that women in her tribe have practiced for centuries.

35

## MAKE ART IN YOUR COUNTRY

Nangura has lived a life that is probably very different from yours. She has never traveled far from her village. Her days are marked by the rising and setting of the sun. She doesn't have electric lights or a television to fill her nights. She spends much of her time outside in nature, and her needs are simple. But it is interesting to hear of what she wants for children. Her hopes for young people are not very different from what parents everywhere want for their children.

*I want the children to learn, so that they can know the good way for their life. Education is important. It is different here. Our children need to learn how to read and write, so they can make a better life.*

As she considers what words of wisdom she could give to all of you who read this book, she smiles shyly, as if something magical is happening to her. Despite the beauty and peacefulness of her way of life, she doesn't feel worthy to give such an important message. But the beauty of her heart shines through, and she offers these words to you.

*Hello, children. I greet you as you read these stories about all the different countries and different peoples. I don't have many words for you. I just hope you make many things, all that you want to make. I hope that you make art in your country!*

*Nangura with her daughter*

## A BASKET FOR YOUR THINGS

You can make a lovely basket out of colored construction paper.

For this activity, you will need:
- At least three sheets of differently colored heavy construction paper.
- A pair of scissors, a pencil, a ruler, and a roll of clear tape.

**Step 1.** Cut the paper into at least twenty 1-inch strips. Lay out half of the strips side by side on a work table. Secure the ends of the paper strips to the table with tape.

**Step 2.** Weave the other strips under and over the strips you've taped down. You may find it easier to weave the strips of paper if you lightly moisten your finger tip. Repeat this step until all the strips are woven together into a checkerboard pattern.

**Step 3.** Apply a long strip of tape along each edge of your woven square. Now, carefully pull the woven sheets up from the table. Turn the sheet over and apply a long strip of tape along each edge of the other side. Cut off the excess tape from all sides.

**Step 4.** Draw a diagonal line from one corner to the opposite corner. Do the same between the other two corners. Now, apply a long strip of tape along each of these lines so the line is in the center of the tape.

**Step 5.** Measure from the center of your sheet (where the two lines cross) out toward each corner. Make a pencil mark at about 2½ inches. Now, with your scissors cut along each line (down the center of the tape) to your pencil mark.

**Step 6.** Fold the loose pieces in toward the center and tape them together to form a basket. Can you think of ways to add a handle or a lid to your basket?

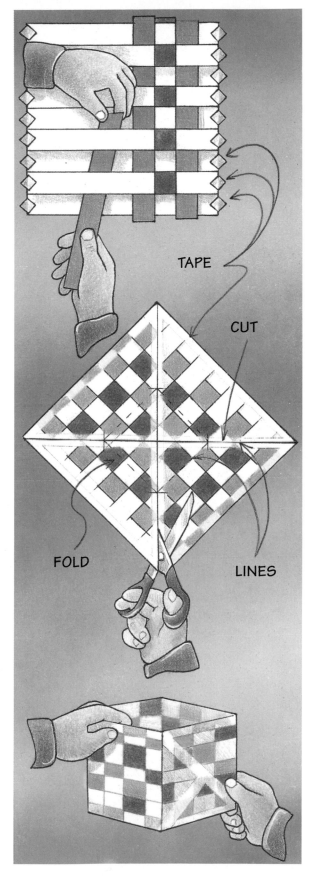

TAPE

CUT

FOLD

LINES

# TSEPO TSHOLA
## of Lesotho

### THE LESOTHO LAND AND PEOPLE

At the far southern tip of Africa lies the mountain kingdom of Lesotho (le-SOH-toh). It is surrounded on all sides by the nation of South Africa, but the two countries are very different from each other. Lesotho was once a colony, but it is now an independent nation. The people of Lesotho, called the Basotho (bah-SOH-toh), come from many tribes. Together they have built a nation that has a rich mixture of traditions. Lesotho is a country of small towns and villages and no large cities.

Lesotho is one of the most beautiful places in Africa, with rolling hills, lush valleys, clean rivers, and the towering Mulati Mountains. Almost everyone in the country is a farmer. They grow maize (a type of corn), sorghum, wheat, peas, beans, and barley. As you travel out into the countryside, you see that the way of life there is not very different from what it was hundreds of years ago. Donkeys pull carts down dirt roads. People pass by on horseback, and you see very few cars.

*"I can't explain the feeling I get when I'm singing to people. A spiritual power comes over me and I just get lost in it."*

—Tsepo Tshola

*A Lesotho farming village*

Over thousands of years the tribes that now live in Lesotho migrated south from northern and central Africa. In recent times wars throughout those regions have scattered a number of tribes. So, much of Lesotho's population arrived here as refugees. Despite the turmoil they have lived through and the differences in their heritages, the Basotho people live peacefully together.

*A Basotho child*

One tradition that is shared by all the tribal people of Lesotho is a reverence for ancestors. As do many other people of Africa, the Basotho believe that people become spiritual messengers to God after they die. Many prayers and rituals center on the tribe's ancestors. Visiting a graveyard in Lesotho is a unique experience. The graves are brightly decorated, and the living speak to the dead as though they were still alive.

The Basotho traditionally measure time by the phases of the moon and the changes in the seasons. Tribal life follows the rhythm of nature, because the planting, nurturing, and harvesting of food is their main occupation. Even today, in the countryside of Lesotho, people speak of time in terms of the movement of the sun and the moon, not in terms of clocks and calendars. Many traditional celebrations are held in connection with seasonal changes. Others revolve around births, weddings, and deaths. The Basotho do not think of these events as religious ceremonies. They say that they are simply celebrations of nature and human life.

Singing and making music are the strongest and most joyous traditional expressions of the Basotho people. Families sing together to celebrate, to mourn, and simply for the joy of singing. They are not timid about their music. It pours out of their hearts and souls. There is a magical quality to it that deeply touches the listener as well as the performer.

*A traditional Lesotho home*

39

Tsepo's friends

Tsepo Tshola *(t'see-POH CHOH-lah)* lives in the land of Lesotho. His mother is from the Maphuthing *(mah-POO-ting)* tribe. His father is from the Ndebeli *(n'deh-BELL-ee)* tribe. Tsepo is 39 years old, but he possesses the joy of a child. Tsepo has three sisters, two brothers, and another brother who passed away.

His childhood was happy, with a loving family who prayed together and shared lots of laughter. His mother grew fresh vegetables in her garden, and fruit trees surrounded his house.

*We didn't have a lot of things. We played outside with balls made of rags. We'd kick them around. We didn't have money to buy a real football (soccer ball). But we weren't poor, no way. We had everything we needed. We had lots of love and lived in a beautiful, natural place. My friends and I had so much fun. I still see them and hang out with them whenever I go home.*

Music became the focus of Tsepo's life at a very early age. His mother would lead the children in singing spiritual songs.

*My mother tells me I was ten when my voice really began to come to me. As a family we sang together all the time. Outside, inside, morning, and night. Happy times and sad times, there always seemed to be a song to sing. Someone would just start, usually my mom, and we would all just join in.*

Tsepo's mother, who is a *sangoma*, or traditional healer, has always been the bright light of his life. His natural joy comes from her belief in him, and his spiritual strength is a reflection of hers.

*When my mother makes a blessing for you, you can feel it in every part of your body. She is so beautiful, so loving, and so powerful. She lifted me up as a child, and she still lifts me up today.*

Tsepo's mom

Tsepo and his niece

Looking out from the front porch of Tsepo's childhood home, you can see valleys and mountains in the distance. At sunrise and sunset the colors on the hills are an electric orange. The pace is slow and easy in his neighborhood. Friends and neighbors wander up to talk and trade jokes. Kids laugh and run in the street. If you saw their villages you might think of the people as poor, but the people are not worried about their future. Families take care of each other, and life goes on as it always has.

At his home, where his mother still lives, is a small graveyard where his father, brother, and wife are buried. When Tsepo comes home he always takes time to go there and talk with each of his missing family members. He laughs and jokes and prays with them.

*I miss them all, especially my beautiful wife. But I know I'll be with them again. Until then, they can hear me talking and singing to them.*

Although his singing has taken him around the world, his home in Lesotho is where he returns as often as possible to renew his spirit, to be close to his family, and to sing the songs of his youth.

*The countryside around Tsepo's home*

## THE VOICE OF FREEDOM

Tsepo Tshola is a singer, a poet, a song-writer, and a performer. As a child he was just another small town kid who liked to sing. Today, Tsepo is a world-renowned musical artist. He has achieved success because he believed in himself and his talents. He never stopped trying to achieve his goals.

*When I was 16 I really got into singing. At 17 I began writing songs. In the beginning it wasn't easy. I sang other people's songs from the radio, Stevie Wonder songs, James Brown stuff, the blues. It was really frustrating to sing other people's songs when I could write my own.*

*Tsepo singing*

By the time Tsepo was in his early twenties the music scene in South Africa was starting to come alive. Out of the black townships, where black South Africans were segregated, a whole new style of music was emerging. It was a combination of traditional and modern music that was unlike anything heard before.

*The inspiration to sing my own music came from hearing the new style of music that grew here in the 1970s. Lots of music groups were formed. The music scene seemed to blossom overnight.*

Tsepo and a friend from Lesotho formed a band called Sankomota. In the beginning they could not find much work, but they were happy to be playing their own music. Their audiences grew, and eventually they released an album called *Dreams Do Come True*. The album *was* a dream come true for Tsepo.

Since then Tsepo has played in many different towns and cities throughout Africa. He has also toured in Europe and the United States.

*I can't explain the feeling I get when I'm singing to peo-ple. A spiritual power comes over me and I just get lost in it.*

Sankomota went on to record two more very

*Tsepo in traditional dress*

*Tsepo sings for joy*

successful albums, *The Writing's on the Wall* and *Exploration*. Tsepo's booming voice and joyful performances have become a symbol of black Africa's struggle for freedom. These are some of the words to his hit song *Stop the War*, which has become a healing anthem in South Africa:

> *This world needs love to keep peace alive.*
> *So let love be king, then peace will reign.*
> *Stop the war, hey, hey. Stop the war, hey, hey.*

Recently, Tsepo stopped performing with the group and now records and tours on his own. His new album is called *The Village Pope.*

*I am still the number one fan of Sankomota and am missing the group so much. My heart remains with them.*

Tsepo has come a long way from his family home in the mountains of Lesotho. His beautiful music and dedication to peace have made him a hero in southern Africa. But his fame hasn't changed the warmth in his heart. When he walks into a room in his traditional robes, laughing, calling out greetings, and hugging friends, you know he still has the same generous spirit that he did as a boy.

43

## LET IT SHINE

Tsepo's success has not been an accident. He was born with talent, but he worked very hard to develop it. He faced difficult times in his early days as a performer. Even now as a very successful singer, he still must do things he doesn't enjoy. But that is balanced by the joy he feels singing and the happiness he brings to others.

Tsepo believes that everyone has something beautiful to offer to other people, whether as an artist, a scientist, an athlete, a business person, or any other occupation. He believes that your future success is already in you waiting to be expressed.

*God has put power in you. You have got it. Take it out and show it, through every kind of talent you can develop: music, writing, painting, dancing or anything else. And he has put love in you. Let it shine.*

If you compare yourself to others you may overlook how unique you are and how much you have to offer. When Tsepo started performing, he could have compared himself to all the great singers in the world and given up after thinking about how far he had to go. Instead, he looked at himself, at what he had to offer, and at what he had to learn.

*If you look at yourself you will see that you are always the best. A living miracle.*

# ACTIVITY PAGE

## SING IT YOUR WAY

Tsepo sings in his own unique way. You can, too. You don't have to know a lot about music to sing.

For this activity, all you need is your voice and a song.

**Step 1.** Pick out a record, tape, or CD with one of your favorite songs on it.

**Step 2.** Listen to the song a few times. Concentrate on the words and the music, and the emotions of the singer.

**Step 3.** Write the words down on a piece of paper. You will have to stop the song and start it over several times to catch all of the words and write them down.

**Step 4.** Turn off the music and practice singing the song. Do this a few times.

**Step 5.** Turn the music back on and sing along to the recording. Keep the volume low enough so you can hear yourself sing. Sing the way you want to sing. Feel the meaning of the words. Sing with all your heart. Sing out to the world! Do this step over and over until you feel you've found your own unique singing style. If you want to, dress up in a costume and perform your song for your family and friends. Have fun!

# GLOSSARIZED INDEX

A portion of the proceeds from the sale of this book go to the Rainbow Warrior Fund (administered by the Tides Foundation) for the preservation of native cultures and the environment. These are some of the organizations we support:

The Huichol Cultural Center, Santiago, Mexico
Lighthawk: The Environmental Air Force, Santa Fe, New Mexico
Native Lifeways: Oneida Nation, Amherst, New York

## COMMUNICATE

Let us know what you think. Write to the artists. Send poetry, pictures, stories, whatever. Send your name and address. We will put you on our mailing list. Write, right now!

Rainbow Warrior
P.O. Box 9858
Santa Fe, New Mexico 87504

## EXTREMELY WEIRD SERIES

*A*ll of the titles are written by Sarah Lovett, 8½" x 11", 48 pages, $9.95 paperback, $14.95 hardcover, with color photographs and illustrations.

Extremely Weird Bats
Extremely Weird Birds
Extremely Weird Endangered Species
Extremely Weird Fishes
Extremely Weird Frogs
Extremely Weird Insects
Extremely Weird Mammals
Extremely Weird Micro Monsters
Extremely Weird Primates
Extremely Weird Reptiles
Extremely Weird Sea Creatures
Extremely Weird Snakes
Extremely Weird Spiders

## X-RAY VISION SERIES

*E*ach title in the series is 8½" x 11", 48 pages, $9.95 paperback, with color photographs and illustrations, and written by Ron Schultz.

Looking Inside the Brain
Looking Inside Cartoon Animation
Looking Inside Caves and Caverns
Looking Inside Sports Aerodynamics
Looking Inside Sunken Treasure
Looking Inside Telescopes and the Night Sky

## THE KIDDING AROUND TRAVEL GUIDES

*A*ll of the titles listed below are 64 pages and $9.95 paperbacks, except for *Kidding Around the National Parks* and *Kidding Around Spain*, which are 108 pages and $12.95 paperbacks.

Kidding Around Atlanta
Kidding Around Boston, 2nd ed.
Kidding Around Chicago, 2nd ed.
Kidding Around the Hawaiian Islands
Kidding Around London
Kidding Around Los Angeles
Kidding Around the National Parks
  of the Southwest
Kidding Around New York City, 2nd ed.
Kidding Around Paris
Kidding Around Philadelphia
Kidding Around San Diego
Kidding Around San Francisco
Kidding Around Santa Fe
Kidding Around Seattle
Kidding Around Spain
Kidding Around Washington, D.C., 2nd ed.

## MASTERS OF MOTION SERIES

*E*ach title in the series is 10¼" x 9", 48 pages, $9.95 paperback, with color photographs and illustrations.

How to Drive an Indy Race Car
  David Rubel
How to Fly a 747
  Tim Paulson
How to Fly the Space Shuttle
  Russell Shorto

## THE KIDS EXPLORE SERIES

*E*ach title is written by kids for kids by the Westridge Young Writers Workshop, 7" x 9", and $9.95 paperback, with photographs and illustrations by the kids.

Kids Explore America's Hispanic Heritage
112 pages

Kids Explore America's African American Heritage 128 pages

Kids Explore the Gifts of Children with Special Needs 128 pages

Kids Explore America's Japanese American Heritage 144 pages

## ENVIRONMENTAL TITLES

Habitats: *Where the Wild Things Live*
Randi Hacker and Jackie Kaufman
8½" x 11", 48 pages, color illustrations, $9.95 paper

The Indian Way: *Learning to Communicate with Mother Earth*
Gary McLain
7" x 9", 114 pages, two-color illustrations, $9.95 paper

Rads, Ergs, and Cheeseburgers: *The Kids' Guide to Energy and the Environment*
Bill Yanda
7" x 9", 108 pages, two-color illustrations, $13.95 paper

The Kids' Environment Book: *What's Awry and Why*
Anne Pedersen
7" x 9",192 pages, two-color illustrations, $13.95 paper

## BIZARRE & BEAUTIFUL SERIES

A spirited and fun investigation of the mysteries of the five senses in the animal kingdom.

Each title in the series is 8½" x 11", $9.95 paperback, $14.95 hardcover, with color photographs and illustrations throughout.

**Bizarre & Beautiful Ears**
**Bizarre & Beautiful Eyes**
**Bizarre & Beautiful Feelers**
**Bizarre & Beautiful Noses**
**Bizarre & Beautiful Tongues**

## RAINBOW WARRIOR SERIES

What is a Rainbow Warrior Artist? It is a person who strives to live in harmony with the Earth and all living creatures, and who tries to better the world while living his or her life in a creative way.

Each title is written by Reavis Moore with a foreword by LeVar Burton, and is 8½" x 11", 48 pages, $14.95 hardcover, with color photographs and illustrations.

**Native Artists of Africa**
**Native Artists of North America**
**Native Artists of Europe**

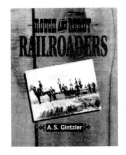

## ROUGH AND READY SERIES

Learn about the men and women who settled the American West. Explore the myths and legends about these courageous individuals and learn about the environmental, cultural, and economic legacies they left to us.

Each title in the series is written by A. S. Gintzler and is 48 pages, 8½" x 11", $12.95 hardcover, with two-color illustrations and duotone archival photographs.

**Rough and Ready Cowboys**
**Rough and Ready Homesteaders**
**Rough and Ready Loggers**

**Rough and Ready Outlaws & Lawmen**
**Rough and Ready Prospectors**
**Rough and Ready Railroaders**

## AMERICAN ORIGINS SERIES

Many of us are the third and fourth generation of our families to live in America. Learn what our great-great-grandparents experienced when they arrived here and how much of our lives are still intertwined with theirs.

Each title is 48 pages, 8½" x 11", $12.95 hardcover, with two-color illustrations and duotone archival photographs.

**Tracing Our English Roots**
**Tracing Our French Roots**
**Tracing Our German Roots**
**Tracing Our Irish Roots**

**Tracing Our Italian Roots**
**Tracing Our Japanese Roots**
**Tracing Our Jewish Roots**
**Tracing Our Polish Roots**